A **SporTellers**™ Book

FEAR ON ICE

EARLE RICE, JR.

A Pacemaker® Program

Fearon Education
a division of
David S. Lake Publishers
Belmont, California

SporTellers™

Senior development editor: Christopher Ransom Miller
Content editor: Carol B. Whiteley
Production editor: Mary McClellan
Design manager: Eleanor Mennick
Illustrator: Bob Haydock
Cover: Bob Haydock

ISBN–0–8224–6476–4
Library of Congress Catalog Card Number: 80–82984
Printed in the United States of America.
1.9 8 7 6 5 4 3

Contents

New Kid in Camp *1*

It was the first day of September and the first official day of training camp. It was also the first day of Neal Calder's professional ice hockey career—a day he had dreamed about for a long, long time.

The clear Minnesota air felt cool against his face when he stepped off the bus. As he looked around, a short, strong-looking man with warm brown eyes walked up to him. The man held out his hand. "You must be Calder," he said. "You look just like your pictures. My name is Frank Slater. Most everyone calls me 'Gutsy,' though. It's left over from my playing days. I'm the team trainer for the Oakland Traders. The coach sent me to give you a lift out to camp."

Neal shook the trainer's hand. He said, "You're right. I'm Neal Calder. Glad to meet you, Gutsy."

The trainer jammed a fresh cigar in his mouth and bit down on it. Speaking out of one side of his mouth, he said, "Same here, Calder. Glad to meet you." Then he reached for one of Neal's bags. "Let me give you a hand with your stuff. My station wagon is that green one."

Gutsy and Neal each put a bag in the back of the wagon and climbed in up front. Gutsy started the engine and wheeled off down the road to the camp.

As the car moved along, the last of the fall leaves fell slowly toward the ground. Gutsy watched them. Then he said, "The word at camp is that you're going to be hockey's next superstar." He smiled. "Anything to that, kid?" Gutsy already knew about Neal the hockey player. But now he wanted to find out about Neal the man.

Neal smiled. "I'm just going to play the game one day at a time. And each day I'll try to put the puck in the net."

Neal Calder wasn't much on blowing his own horn. But he knew he was right up there with the best hockey players in the country. From the first day he tied on a pair of skates, he belonged to the ice. That was at the age of five. Now, at 21, he had grown into a hockey player's hockey player. He was young, tough, and—most important—smart.

"I guess you're not the talking kind," Gutsy said. "But I know your record. You were a real big star at Denver." He waited for Neal to say something.

"I did all right, I guess," Neal said.

Neal had played four years for the University of Denver. And he had done better than just all right. He had broken every college hockey record in the book. But he knew that he didn't have to tell Gutsy that.

"OK, kid," Gutsy went on. "I won't press you about your past. But tell me this: What kind of shape are you in now?"

"Pretty fair, I'd say," Neal answered. "Why do you ask?"

Gutsy rolled his cigar to the other side of his mouth. "Because most of the guys from last year's team reported to camp about a week early," he said. "They wanted to get a head start on getting into shape. So, unless you're in real good shape, some of them will probably have a leg up on you."

Neal turned to look at Gutsy. "Maybe," he said. "But I don't think so."

"I hope not." Gutsy turned onto a winding dirt road. Then he stopped. "Listen, kid. What I'm trying to tell you is this. If you're half as good as they say you are, you're going to be taking another player's job away from him. And every guy in camp knows that his job may be up for grabs. So every player on the team will be coming after you."

Neal let Gutsy's words sink in for a minute. Then he said, "Thanks for telling me all this, Gutsy. But I think I can take care of myself. I'll be all right."

Gutsy looked hard at Neal. Then he started the station wagon moving again. "I hope so, kid," he said. "I sure hope so."

CHAPTER

The First Day 2

When the green station wagon reached the Traders' training camp, Gutsy stopped it in front of the coach's office. A young kid who helped around the camp took Neal's bags and said he would put them in Neal's room. Then Gutsy and Neal went in to see Grady Hall, winning coach for the Oakland Traders. Coach Hall looked up from his desk. "Good morning, Gutsy," he said. "I see you found someone waiting at the bus stop."

Gutsy put out his cigar in the wastebasket. "Right, Coach," he said. "Our superstar from Denver."

The coach looked at Neal through hard blue eyes. He didn't speak for what seemed like years. Finally he said, "We don't have any

superstars in this camp. Just team players.
Remember that, kid, and you and I will get
along fine."

Neal felt like slipping out through a crack
in the floor. Then he got mad. "You remember
something too," he said. "You guys are the
ones talking about superstars—not me. I'll do
my talking out on the ice."

At that, the coach laughed. And it seemed
to Neal that the whole room shook with the
sound. Grady Hall was a big man, with bright
red hair and a full red face. When he laughed,
people knew it. And when he spoke, most

people listened. "You said that pretty well, kid," Grady told Neal when he finally stopped laughing. "I like your stuff." Then he stood up—all nine yards of him—and offered his big hand to Neal. "Welcome to the Oakland Traders," he said.

The Oakland Traders had been last year's champion—the Gilbert Cup winner—in the Pacific Hockey League. Now Neal was one of them. Smiling, he shook Grady's hand. "Thanks," he said. The first ice of the new season had been broken.

But just as Neal began to feel easy, Coach Hall ended the meeting. "I've got work to do. Gutsy, show the kid the camp. And try to keep him out of trouble." Hall's big laugh shook the room again as Gutsy and Neal headed out the door.

Neal's and Gutsy's first stop was at the locker room. There, Neal was fitted for skates and a black and orange Trader uniform. After that, Gutsy showed Neal around the rest of the camp and had him meet most of the other players. They seemed OK. But no one had much to say. Then came lunch, followed by an afternoon visit with the team doctor. The doctor found Neal in great shape. At a hard 190 pounds, Neal Calder was ready to play hockey.

As Gutsy and Neal left the doctor's office, Gutsy drew Neal to the side. "OK, kid. That's it for today. Workouts start tomorrow. Be at the rink at eight o'clock sharp. The coach likes his players to be on time."

"Right, Gutsy. And thanks for all your help today." Neal waved a hand at the trainer and started to turn away.

But Gutsy put a hand on Neal's arm. "One more thing. The doctor says you're in great shape. And I can tell you can handle yourself OK. But don't forget what I told you this morning." Smoke poured out of Gutsy's ever-present cigar. "Some of those guys you're going to lock horns with tomorrow are real animals. So from here on out, keep your head up and your eyes open." Then the trainer's eyes began to sparkle. "And don't back down from anyone!"

When Neal got to his room, he opened his bags and started to put away his clothes. Packed between his shirts was a picture of him and his wife Amy having a picnic in the backyard of their Berkeley, California, house.

Neal smiled as he put the picture on a small table beside his bed. He loved playing hockey. But he hated being away from Amy. While he finished unpacking, he thought about all the fun they had together. Then he headed for dinner.

That night, tired from a full day, Neal went to bed early. He was looking forward to what the next day would bring. And sleep came quickly.

But for the man across the hall from Neal, sleep wouldn't come. So the man lay on his bed, thinking far into the night. He thought about what he would do to Neal Calder. Tomorrow. Out on the ice.

CHAPTER 3

Eddie Blair

The next morning, Coach Hall showed up at the ice rink at eight o'clock on the dot. Gutsy Slater was with him. And all but one of the players were already there. Everyone on the team knew that the coach liked his players to be on time.

As the first day of training began, Coach Hall called the men into the gray and brown locker room. While the players sat around on wood benches, the coach walked back and forth in front of them. He talked as he walked. "Hockey is a tough game," he began. "And that's the way my teams play it. When you play for me, you play tough!" He stopped and studied his players' faces for a minute. A few of the men looked at the floor. A few nodded.

Coach Hall went on. "Last year, we won big in the Pacific Hockey League. We won by playing *tough*. This year, we are going to be number one again—by playing the same way." Coach Hall moved to the middle of the room. He looked at the players one by one. "Now, listen close to what I've got to say. If you don't remember anything else after today, remember this: If you can't beat the other team in a street fight, you can't beat them on the ice. So, the first time someone pushes you out there, you better push back. And you better be ready to fight at the drop of a glove. *That's* what wins hockey games. And that's what will take us to the top again this year. Any questions?"

Before anyone could talk, the door to the locker room swung open. The missing player walked in. He was a tall, big-armed man whom Neal Calder had not yet met. The man's name was Eddie Blair.

Coach Hall shot a hard look at Blair, as the player found a place on the bench. "So nice of you to join us this morning, Eddie," the coach said. His voice sounded sharp enough to cut glass. "I do hope we didn't put you to any trouble. I mean, we didn't get you up too early now, did we?"

Eddie Blair had been awake most of the night. Sleep had not come until early morning. So when his alarm clock had started ringing, he had turned it off to get a few minutes more sleep. But he ended up sleeping a lot longer than he had planned. Now he was late—and in trouble with the coach.

"Sorry I'm late, Grady," Blair said. The room was still again as every player waited to find out what the coach would say—and do.

"I know you're sorry, Eddie," Coach Hall said. "And because I know you're sorry, I'm going to take it easy on you." The coach smiled while he talked to Eddie. But Eddie guessed that the smile wasn't a sign that the big man was happy. He was sure of it when the coach spoke again. "Ten fast turns around the ice should help make up for what you've missed by being late. And I want you to skate them at the end of our workout."

Eddie didn't like what he heard. He knew he would feel bad at the end of the day. But he knew he had the added work coming. "Yes, sir," he said, waiting for the coach to start talking about the morning workout. But Coach Hall wasn't finished talking about players who come late.

"I've got one more thing to say, so listen good. Anyone who shows up late after today will get 20 fast trips around the ice. I don't want anyone on this team who can't follow the rules. I only took it easy on Eddie this time because he isn't as young as he used to be." The coach's hard smile came back. "Right, Eddie?"

"You and me both, Coach," Eddie said with a hard smile of his own.

Coach Hall and Eddie Blair went back a long way together. Years before, Eddie's father had been an oil worker in California. In 1947, when oil was found in Alberta, Canada, the Blair family had moved there. Eddie was only six, but he had started playing junior hockey. Grady Hall was his coach then. And he had been his coach ever since.

The two men had weathered some long, hard years together. They were both good. Very good. But they had never quite made it to the big time—the National Hockey League. Now they were both nearing the end of their careers. Coach Hall planned to leave the Traders after the coming season ended. Eddie knew that, and he wanted to take over as coach. He knew he would be a good coach. But to be named to the job, he had to last one more year as a player for the Traders. He wasn't at all sure that he would last the season. And Coach Hall wasn't the kind to carry anyone who couldn't cut it anymore. Friends or not.

Now the coach ended the meeting saying, "OK, guys, that's it. Get your stuff on and hit the ice." He moved to a corner as the players tied on their skates and pulled on freshly washed uniforms.

Soon the last few men headed for the rink. Eddie Blair was with them. As Blair walked out the door, the coach called him back. "Wait a minute, Eddie. I want to talk to you," he said.

Eddie turned and went back. "What about, Grady?"

"About you, Eddie," the coach said. "I've been watching you this last week—ever since you showed up in camp. Seems like you've really slowed down out there. You're not making the plays like you used to. Something the matter?"

"Not really," Eddie answered. He rubbed his arm as he talked. "It's just taking me a little longer to work into shape this year. That's all. I'll be in great shape real soon."

"I hope so, Eddie," the coach said. "Because you know I never carry any dead weight."

"Don't worry, Grady. My weight is still very much among the living," Eddie said. "Anything more?"

"Yes," the coach answered. He looked Eddie square in the face. "How are your hands? Still as quick as ever?"

Eddie returned the coach's look. "My hands are as fast as they ever were," he said. "And that's very fast."

"Seeing is believing," Coach Hall went on. "So show me. Go out there and do a number on the new kid."

"You mean Neal Calder?"

"That's right, Eddie. I mean Neal Calder."

Eddie's face started moving into a long smile. "I've been thinking about nothing but that for days," he said.

Roommates 4

Coach Hall had wondered about two things before he sent Eddie Blair after Neal Calder. He had wondered what kind of stuff the new kid was really made of. And he had wondered if his old friend still owned the fastest pair of hands in the West. He had decided it would take a fight to get the answers to those questions.

As soon as he reached the rink, Coach Hall called for the first team scrimmage. He told half the players to slip orange shirts over their black uniforms and the other half to stay the way they were. When the two teams were ready, they faced each other on the ice. Neal Calder and Eddie Blair were playing on different teams.

No one spoke as every man waited for the puck to drop. Sticks were ready to move. Then Coach Hall, who was acting as referee, dropped the puck at center ice. And the fun began.

The sounds of loud voices and wood against wood filled the air. Both teams were out to win. And Neal Calder and Eddie Blair were out to show they were winners. Five minutes into the scrimmage, Neal picked the puck off the stick of a forward on the other team. With a quick move to his left, then another to his right, he slipped around the forward. Controlling the puck as if it were tied to his stick, he flashed off down the ice. One of his own forwards followed the play. The forward hung off to Neal's left and a little behind him. Neal raced in over the other team's blue line. The puck moved with him toward a sure score.

Suddenly, Eddie Blair came out on defense to cut him off. "I'll take care of this superstar," he shouted at his team's other defenseman. "You watch out for that guy on the point!"

As Neal started to shoot for the goal, Eddie stopped short, trying to block Neal's shot. But Neal didn't shoot. Instead, he dropped off

a pass to his forward. Since Eddie wasn't quick enough to play the puck, the way Neal had, he had played the man. And he had been burned. The puck went speeding past Eddie to one of Neal's forwards. The forward caught the hard rubber puck on the toe of his stick with a cracking sound. He fired it hard toward the net. Toward the net, but a little wide.

Neal was ready when the puck came rocketing back to him. As soon as he had passed off, he had shown Eddie Blair two quick moves and had gone around him. Then he had planted himself and waited. Now, as the puck shot forward, Neal reached out with his stick and touched it. The puck changed course and dropped into the net. Neal lifted his arms and stick high over his head, the way hockey players do when they score.

Neal was happy. But he didn't have long to enjoy his big moment. The blow came suddenly—from behind. And the force of it sent Neal flying through the air. Then the ice came up fast to meet him. Neal hit the ice hard and slid along it for yards. When he finally came to a stop, his face burned. Slowly he turned over and sat up. Then he waited for his head to clear. He felt his back where the stick had found its mark. It hurt like a son of a gun. Someone was going to pay for that, Neal told himself.

That someone was Eddie Blair. When Neal looked up the big man was standing over him. His gloves were off, and his hands looked ready for a fight.

Neal got to his feet fast. He spoke to Blair. "You the one who cracked me with a stick?"

Eddie smiled. "What do *you* think, kid?"

Neal's answer came suddenly. In one move he tore off his gloves and swung his left hand toward the waiting player's face. Eddie slid inside it. Then he banged a hard left of his own into Calder's middle. Neal came back with a short right that hit its mark. Blood fell from Eddie's nose and covered the ice below him with red spots.

Three other players moved forward to try to break up the fight. But Coach Hall stopped them. "Let them go! Let's see what they can do," he ordered. The players backed off. The whole team waited while the men pounded each other.

Both men landed heavy blows. But neither would let himself be knocked to the ice. They stood toe to toe and skate to skate. And they kept fighting until they grew too tired to lift their arms anymore.

When it was all over, both men were still standing. Both were cut in many places. But neither man had won. As several players helped the two men to the locker room, Coach Hall knew the answers to his questions. And they were the right answers.

Later that night, Gutsy spoke to Neal. "You did real well out there today, kid. Real well."

Neal smiled through lips a little the worse for wear. "Thanks," he said. "But it's not over yet."

And it wasn't. Not by a long shot. In almost every workout, Eddie Blair and Neal Calder traded blows. Each man tried for a clear win. But neither got it.

The days passed slowly. Both men hurt from all the fighting. Neal was young, though, as well as strong. So his hockey playing was as good as ever. But the wear and tear on Eddie's aging body didn't help his hockey playing at all. The players started to whisper that Eddie Blair wasn't going to make the team that year.

Then a strange thing happened. Near the end of training, two of the other Trader defensemen got hurt on the same play during a scrimmage. They would be out for most of the season. Coach Hall was forced to sign Eddie Blair for one more year.

On the last day of training camp, Coach Hall called Eddie and Neal to his office. "Since you two will be playing together on defense, you're going to have to learn to work together.

So I've decided to help you out." The red-haired man looked at Eddie and then at Neal. "I've decided to make you two roommates when the team is on the road."

Eddie Blair jumped up. But Neal spoke first. "There is no way you can make me room with that man," he said. "I just won't."

Coach Hall moved forward and tapped his finger on Neal's chest. "You'll do anything I tell you to, kid," he said. His voice was low, but as strong as ever. "I'm running this show. And I'm telling you you're roommates—or you're off the team!"

CHAPTER **5**

Hot Dog with Mustard

"You're on your own until Friday the thirteenth. Be at the Oakland Coliseum Arena at six o'clock sharp!" With those words, Coach Hall ended five long, hard weeks of training. Every player on the team headed for home.

Amy Hansen-Calder met Neal at the Oakland Airport and drove to their house in the Berkeley hills close by. Neal was happy to be with Amy. But on the way home, they passed the coliseum. As he watched it move behind him, Neal thought about his career in professional hockey. His career would soon be over if he couldn't bring himself to room with Eddie Blair. Neal stayed lost in thought for most of the ride home.

After dinner that night, Neal and Amy washed the dishes. Neal didn't say anything was wrong. But he really didn't talk very much. Finally, Amy had to say something. "OK. I know something is troubling you. Would it help to talk about it?"

Neal told her the whole story. How Eddie Blair dogged his every move on the ice. How Blair had tried to keep Neal from being able to stay on the team. How the game of hockey that Neal loved had turned from tough and fast to cheap and dirty. And most of all how Neal had grown to hate Eddie Blair.

Neal had stormed around the kitchen while he talked. Now he dropped into a chair. He looked at Amy. "I know we both decided I should stick with hockey. But I told the coach I'd leave the team before I'd room with a man like Blair."

Amy walked over to Neal and sat in the chair next to him. "I'd hate to see you give up everything you've worked so hard for. Why don't you wait for the first game and ask Coach Hall to think about it again?"

Neal said he would. And he and Amy tried hard to keep hockey out of their minds for the next few days. They saw their friends. Went to movies. Read and talked. Then, suddenly, it was Friday the thirteenth. It was opening day of the Traders' season.

Neal said good-bye to Amy in the stands and went straight to the locker room. Coach Hall sat in a corner as he watched his players dress for the game. Neal went over and explained why it would be better for the team if he and Eddie Blair didn't room together.

Coach Hall blew up. "Don't come at me with that stuff now, kid," he said as he stood up. "I don't have time for it. I've got a hockey game to win tonight." He turned to walk away.

Neal grabbed his arm. "Then maybe you'll just have to try winning it without me," he said.

The coach was so angry his face turned a deeper red. He looked down at Neal. "If you don't play tonight, I'll hit you with a fine like you wouldn't believe. And you'll forget how to skate before you ever get to play hockey again!" He stormed out of the room and down the hall.

Neal was really mad. But he decided to sit down on the bench and think things over. The other players looked at him, but they didn't say a word. Finally they went back to getting ready for the game. Neal opened his locker and looked at the fresh, clean uniform hanging inside. Number 16. One part of him wanted to put it on and get set for the game. But the other part said no.

Eddie Blair had come into the locker room. He walked over to the bench and started to open the locker next to Neal's. He tried to make his voice sound the same as always. But it didn't. "The coach says that you may not be getting dressed for the game," he said. "That right?"

Neal's answer was cold. "What does it matter to you?" He started to get up.

Blair put out a hand and touched Neal's arm. "Your playing matters a lot to me," he said. "And to the team. I know I was hard on you during training. But I was afraid you were so good that I'd lose my spot on the team. And hockey's my life. The game is tough. So the only way I know to fight is tough. If those two guys on our team hadn't been hurt, I probably wouldn't be here now. But I am here. And I want to play on the team with you. You're good, kid. Let's be friends. What do you say?"

Neal stood up. "I say no." He turned and walked out.

Outside the locker room, Amy was talking with another woman and a small girl. Amy smiled when she saw Neal. She took him by the hand. "I want you to meet two friends of mine," she said. "This is Carol Blair. And this is Maria." Amy smiled again, and her eyes sparkled. "Carol told me something up in the stands that I thought you might like to hear."

Before Neal could get over his surprise, Carol Blair spoke. "I'm so happy to meet you, Neal. My husband has told me a great deal about you. All good. He really thinks a lot of you, you know."

Neal shook his head. "I'm afraid you have me mixed up with someone else," he said. "What you said just couldn't be true."

Then the little girl pushed forward. In one hand she had a hot dog coated with mustard. In the other hand she had a Traders flag. "My dad says Neal Calder is the best hockey player in the game. And if he says it, it must be true."

Neal looked from the girl to her mother and back again. Then he looked at Amy. "I think I've got a hockey game to play!"

Neal almost flew back into the locker room. Eddie Blair still sat on the bench pulling on his uniform. Neal walked up to Eddie and put out his hand. "That offer of yours still good?"

Eddie took Neal's hand and shook it. "You know it," he said.

Five minutes later, Neal and Eddie were dressed for the game. Together they left the locker room. And together they hit the ice.

CHAPTER 6

Winning

As the Oakland Traders warmed up, crowds of people streamed by the lighted sign outside the coliseum parking lot. The sign said:

HOCKEY TONIGHT
L.A. LIONS vs. OAKLAND TRADERS
8:00 P.M.

With 20 minutes until game time, every seat in the house was filled. The press boxes were also filled. Both teams had returned to their locker rooms after warming up. A few minutes before 8:00, a radio team began its show:

Hello, again, out there! This is Manuel Lazar, and next to me is Ted Baker. We'll be your hockey voices for this first game of the season for the Oakland Traders. Tonight's game against the Los Angeles Lions will be coming to you—LIVE—from the Oakland Coliseum Arena. Ted and I will be back in a minute with a look at the starting players. But first, a moment to. . . .

While the call letters of the radio station were told, Coach Hall said a few words to his team. "OK, guys," he said. "It's time to start earning your keep. Play tough. And play to win. Now get out there and score."

The coach opened the door for his team. With Eddie Blair leading them out, the Traders headed down the hall toward the ice. In seconds, the orange and black colors of the Oakland Traders joined the blue and gold of the Los Angeles Lions in the rink.

The crowd stood to sing "The Star-Spangled Banner." Then everyone was still as the two teams lined up for the face-off. The referee dropped the puck. Sticks cracked together and shouts flew. The new season had started.

The Oakland center won the face-off and banged the puck across the ice to Eddie Blair. Eddie skated it back behind his own net and

Neal followed. "Take it on down," Eddie said to Neal as he passed off the puck to him. "I'll trail the play." Neal nodded and moved fast along the left boards. The Oakland forward line set up in front of him as Manuel Lazar called the play:

Blair sends it to Calder behind the net. Calder skates it out to center ice along the far boards. He passes up to Pearson at left wing. Pearson drops it off to Clyde at center. Clyde shoots. A save! He shoots again. Another save! The puck comes free in front of the net. Clyde knocks it out to Calder. Calder shoots. He SCORES!

The crowd broke into loud shouts and stamped their feet as the Oakland players pounded Neal on the back. Manuel Lazar had to shout to be heard:

What a shot! What a shot! Young Neal Calder has just scored a beautiful goal only 20 seconds into the game. A rocket from the left point. The Oakland Traders lead it 1 to nothing. It looks like it's going to be a big night for Oakland!

Play started up again. But when the first period ended, the score was still 1–0. Then, in the second period, the Lions tied it with a goal by Paul Caron. A few minutes later, Neal put the Traders out in front once more. He picked up a free puck in close and jammed it home. It was 2–1 Traders.

Then Eddie Blair picked up two penalties for fighting. He won the fights but lost out to the referee. The Traders had to play one man short for most of the second period. But Oakland played strong. At the end of the period, the score was still 2–1.

Play moved slowly as the third period started. Then Neal broke it open. Ted Baker called it this way:

Paul Caron grabs the puck for L.A. He passes off to his center. Calder breaks it up. Calder has the puck for the Traders. He's all by himself on a breakaway. He drives for the goal. The Lions' goalie comes out of the net to cut him off. Calder fakes and goes around him. He slides the puck in the net behind the goalie. HAT TRICK FOR NEAL CALDER! His third goal in his first professional hockey game! Oakland has a new superstar!

With the crowd behind them, the Traders kept on scoring. Two more points were added to their side of the board. At the end of the game, Oakland had beaten Los Angeles 5–1. Their new season was starting out where their old one had ended—on top.

Two days later, the Traders won another game at home. Oakland beat San Diego 4–2. Neal made one of the goals. Then the team left town for their first set of games on the road. They played in Portland, Seattle, Fresno, and San Diego. And they won every game. Then they played in Los Angeles, where they tied the Lions 2–2. In the race for the Gilbert Cup, the Traders were right up there.

As the Traders headed toward a winning season, Neal Calder and Eddie Blair became a winning pair. They were a great two-man show on the ice. But they were also friends off the ice. They began to know each other as real people. And when the Traders were at home, the Calders and the Blairs spent a lot of time together. Not only were Neal and Eddie becoming good friends, but Amy Hansen-Calder and Carol Blair were close too.

One Saturday night, the four friends were having dinner together. Half the season was over. And most of the talk at the dinner table was about hockey. Neal and Eddie went over what they planned to do against Los Angeles the next day. The Lions were close behind the Traders in the league standings, so Sunday's game was important.

After talk about the next game ended, the group moved into the living room. Soon they found themselves talking about one another's plans for the years to come. Carol looked a bit sad as she said, "Eddie and I are sure going to miss you two when you go."

Amy looked at her. She said, "What are you talking about, Carol?"

Carol shot a fast look at her husband before answering. "Eddie says that the Boston Bruins will probably call Neal up to the NHL any day now," she said. "Hasn't Neal said anything about it?"

Amy knew that the Oakland Traders were a farm team for the Boston Bruins of the National Hockey League. And that Neal one day would move up to the Bruins. But she and Neal both thought that NHL play was still a year or two away. She said so. But Eddie said no.

"The way Neal is playing these days, the call might even come tomorrow," he said.

Neal laughed. "Come on, Eddie," he said. "That's silly."

"No, it's not," Eddie answered. "Since Carol let the cat out of the bag, I might as well tell the rest. Grady Hall told me that the Bruins are asking about you. The call up to the NHL could come really soon now. I thought he had told you, but I guess not."

Neal wasn't laughing now. "You're kidding," he said.

"No, really," Eddie told him. "And Grady told me something else too. He told me that I've got the inside track for taking over his job. If I stay with the team as a player until the end of the season, I'm in!"

For the rest of the night, the Blairs and the Calders shared their dreams. But the night flew by, and the next day their dreams turned into nightmares.

CHAPTER 7

Getting Even

On Sunday afternoon, the Traders and the Lions met once again in the Oakland Coliseum Arena. Both teams wanted to come out on top. A win for Los Angeles would make the Lions almost even with the Traders in the league standings. An Oakland win would move the Traders out to a safe lead.

At the end of the first period, the score stood at a dead even 1–1. Coach Hall wasn't happy. He stormed up and down the locker room. "What are you guys doing out there? You all look like you're trying to win the 'Mr. Nice Guy of the Year' award," he shouted. "Being nice doesn't win games. From now on, I want to see some hitting out there. Hard hitting. Understand?"

The Oakland Traders did a lot of hitting in the second period. And Eddie Blair did most of it. In almost every play, he sent bodies flying all over the ice. It wasn't long before the Lions hit back. Reggie "Bad Boy" Moyer, defenseman for the Lions, decided Eddie needed to learn a thing or two. The strike came about eight minutes into the second period.

Eddie was racing back into his own end after a free puck. Bad Boy came on like a flash, trying to beat him to it. The two players reached the puck at the same time. And they hit each other head-on, like two speeding trains on the same track. The force of their meeting knocked them both down on the ice. But Bad Boy ended up on top of Eddie. And before Eddie could get up, Moyer banged the handle end of his stick into the back of Eddie's head. It was a cheap, dirty shot that the referee didn't see.

But Neal Calder did.

As the referee called the play dead, Bad Boy Moyer got up. Eddie Blair didn't. Gutsy Slater came out on the ice and raced toward the fallen player. And while he did, Neal Calder went after Moyer. Manuel Lazar called the

fight for the people at home. And he almost kept up with it:

Eddie Blair is down on the ice from the run-in with Bad Boy Moyer. Blair isn't moving. He looks really hurt. Wait a minute now! Neal Calder is racing over to Moyer. The kid is throwing off his gloves—and now he nails Moyer with a smashing left. He follows with another left and a right. Another right. ANOTHER right! And a left and a right. So far, Moyer hasn't been able to strike back at all. The Oakland kid's hands are too fast to follow. Moyer is taking blow after blow. Two more rights by Calder. Moyer goes down. Calder jumps on top of him, still pounding away. You just wouldn't believe what's happening here. Right, Ted?

Ted Baker tried to tell the listeners at home about the sight too:

I've never seen anything like this. Neal Calder is a wild man out there. He's all over Moyer. He's a man gone mad. Someone better break it up—before Calder does Moyer in!

Down on the ice, the two linesmen were finally able to drag Neal off Moyer. When they pulled Neal away, Moyer didn't move. He and Eddie Blair had to be carried off the ice. Then the referee tried to return the arena to some order. He started by throwing Neal Calder out of the game.

In the locker room, Neal found Gutsy with the team doctor taking care of Eddie. Neal looked at the trainer and asked, "How is he?"

Gutsy waved a hand in the air. "He took a bad knock on the head. And he hurt his back in the fall. He'll probably miss a few games. But he'll be OK." Then Gutsy turned toward Neal. "You sure got even for him, kid. You did a good job."

Until that moment, Neal hadn't really thought about his jumping Moyer as getting even. He had only acted in the way that seemed right at the time. Thinking about it for the first time, he said, "Yes, Gutsy, I guess I did." And he and Gutsy both smiled.

Neal was happy that Eddie would be all right. And he was glad that he had been able to get even for a friend. But he didn't stay glad for long. Without Neal and Eddie, the Traders lost to the Lions. That was bad enough. But at the end of the game, Gutsy went to visit the L.A. locker room. When he returned to the Oakland locker room, he looked a little white. He went right over to Neal, who was getting dressed. "Glad I caught you, kid," he said. "I just found out they took Bad Boy Moyer to the hospital. You might want to go on over there. Because. . . ." Gutsy stopped for a minute. Then he said, "Because the guys on the Lions don't think he's going to live."

CHAPTER 8

Playing Scared

Neal and Amy drove right over to the hospital on MacArthur Boulevard. Neal asked the nurse at the desk how Moyer was. She said, "Mr. Moyer is still in surgery. So I don't know. We told his team that we would call them when we know more. But you can wait if you wish. It may be a long while. There's a waiting room outside surgery on the fourth floor. I'll let the doctor know you're there." Neal and Amy went up to the room and began their long wait in worn-out green chairs.

Sounds of rolling beds and running feet could be heard in other parts of the hospital every now and then. But the waiting room stayed still. Neither Neal nor Amy spoke. They just sat there, hoping that the Lions player would make it through the night. While Neal sat with his eyes closed, he tried to fit together the pieces of the bad dream he was caught up in. How had it started?

He remembered seeing Eddie Blair and Bad Boy Moyer fall to the ice. Then Moyer had cracked Eddie with his stick—while Eddie was still down. Neal remembered an angry feeling coming over him. He had to show Moyer that he didn't take that kind of hit lying down. Not when his best friend was the one being hit.

Neal remembered landing the first two or three blows. After that, the fight had no shape or order. He had hit Moyer again and again. He couldn't stop. Something had happened to him out on the ice that had never happened to him before. For a few seconds, he had lost all control over himself. He had become a wild animal let out of some dark forest. And like a wild animal, he had acted without reason.

As Neal thought over what had happened that night, he became frightened. He had always thought that he knew himself well. But now he began to think he didn't know himself at all. There was another side to Neal that had suddenly come to life. It was a side Neal didn't like—one that could try to kill another human being.

While Neal thought and thought into the night, Amy lay sleeping in the wide chair. The first light of morning had just come through the window when a tired doctor opened the door. She looked at Neal and Amy as Amy sat up in her chair. She asked, "Are you the people who came to see about Mr. Moyer?"

"Yes we are," Neal said. He stood up. "How is he, Doctor?"

The doctor smiled a warm smile. "Mr. Moyer is a tough young man. He's been hurt a great deal. But he's going to be fine, just fine."

Neal and Amy hugged each other as the doctor finished speaking. The weight of the world seemed to float right off Neal's back. But in the days to come, the weight was back again. Neal's game was off.

The first sign of trouble came in Seattle. Neal checked a Seattle player off the puck and into the boards. Play stopped. The Seattle man threw down his gloves and started swinging. Neal just grabbed him around the arms and held on. When play started up again, Neal wondered why he had just held on without fighting back. While he was wondering, a Seattle wing stuffed the puck in Oakland's net. Twice more that day, Neal's mind was not on the game. Oakland lost to Seattle 3–1.

Neal kept on having trouble—in Portland, Fresno, and San Diego. When fights started, he didn't fight back. And then he couldn't play well. Oakland lost five games in a row and dropped to second place behind Los Angeles.

Amy tried to help Neal get over the nightmare of his fight with Bad Boy Moyer. But Neal's bad dream stayed with him until Eddie Blair returned to the team. Eddie was all right. And he knew what Neal was going through. He helped Neal along. And for a while, Neal seemed to be getting his game back together. The Traders posted two quick wins at home, and things started looking up.

Then the Traders went to Los Angeles. A win at the L.A. Forum would put Oakland back in first place, and no one knew that better than Coach Hall. Before the game started, he spoke to his team. "Listen, guys. Listen real good. I *want* this hockey game. I will be very angry if we lose. Do you understand me?"

They did. Neal showed some of his early flash, picking up two goals and an assist. And Eddie played tough. With the two men's help, the Traders won and returned to Oakland in first place again.

But something still seemed to be missing from Neal's game. He was playing well. But he wasn't the tough Neal Calder who had first joined the Traders. The job of pointing this out to him fell to Coach Hall. While Neal was dressing for a game with Fresno, the coach talked to him.

"You're not hitting anyone out there, kid," he said. "What are you waiting for?"

Neal looked up. Surprise showed on his face. "I thought I'd been checking pretty hard out there," he said.

Coach Hall shook his head at Neal. "You've been on top of things, sure. But you're not using your hands. You haven't been close to a fight since that Moyer thing. You keep backing down from fights. You know, kid, if you keep it up, those guys out there will run you right off the ice. And I'll put you on the bench. You won't last long in this league playing scared."

Neal finished tying his skate. "I know," he said. "And I'm working on it. But each time I start to swing at a guy, I see Moyer's face in front of me. And remember I almost killed him."

Coach Hall looked hard at Neal. "Forget Moyer," he said. "I want to see some hands at work out there." Then he walked off.

Eddie Blair had been sitting near Neal while Coach Hall spoke. Now he put a hand on his friend's arm. "Don't let it worry you," he said. "You're working on it. When you have a close call like you did with Moyer, it takes time to get back into the game. But you'll do it."

"Thanks, Eddie," Neal said. And he began to think that things really would work out. With Eddie's help, he would get his game back together.

Neal left the locker room feeling better. But the next day, Eddie Blair got the news that he had been sold to the Los Angeles Lions.

CHAPTER

Playing Tough 9

The trip to the airport in the Calder car two days later was a sad one. The Blairs sat in the back seat, trying to think of something happy to say. But no one was in a happy state of mind. Eddie Blair's dream of coaching the Traders was at an end. Neal Calder was losing his good friend. Eddie was the only one who might be able to help Neal return to his old self on the ice. Carol and Amy were losing each other's company. Only Maria was looking forward to the plane ride to Los Angeles.

After the red and orange PSA jet lifted off into the sky, Neal and Amy walked back to the parking lot. Eddie's parting words played over and over again in Neal's mind: "The Moyer thing was a bad time. But it was just one of those things. Put it out of your mind—once and for all. All you need to think about is that hockey is a tough game. And you've got to play it tough!" Those words—play it tough—stayed in Neal's head all the way home.

They were still in his head the following night as he dressed for the game with the Portland Bears. The Bears needed a win in the worst way. With the season winding down, time was running out on their play-off hopes. Only the first four teams in the final standings got to play for the Gilbert Cup. And Portland was number five. They were ready to do anything to get into the play-offs.

One of the things the Bears did was to try to put Neal Calder out of the game. They not only tried, they did. But not in the way they thought they would. The people listening on the radio to Manuel Lazar and Ted Baker heard it this way:

Hello, again, everyone. I'm Manuel Lazar, and with me is Ted Baker. The two of us are set to bring you another fine Oakland Traders hockey game. With Portland looking for

*a play-off spot, we should be in for a great
night. As you probably know, the Traders
are having their troubles holding on to first
place. They could sure use a good game out
of young Neal Calder tonight. But that's
something they haven't been able to get for
quite a while. What about it, Ted?*

Baker answered:

*You're right, Manuel. For some reason, the
kid who used to look like a superstar isn't
pulling his weight anymore. But with Eddie
Blair gone, Calder is going to have to shape
up. And, if he doesn't, the Traders are going
to be in real trouble.*

Down on the ice, the two teams lined up for
the face-off. Neal Calder took up his station
on left defense. Then the referee dropped the
puck. And the game began.

Back on the radio, Manuel Lazar began his
play-by-play:

*Portland wins the face-off. Nils Johnson at
center passes off to Cartier on right wing.
Cartier goes into the Oakland end and takes
the puck behind the net. Johnson is waiting*

out in front. Cartier tries a pass to Johnson. But Calder moves into Johnson from behind and knocks him down. A good move by Calder. Pearson picks up the puck for Oakland and clears it out to Clyde. But the referee stops the play. Offside pass. They will face it off at–wait a minute! HOLD EVERY- THING! There seems to be something start- ing in front of the Oakland net. Cartier is pushing Calder. They both drop their sticks and gloves and put up their hands. Now they are circling each other. Cartier throws a left that misses. Calder starts back with a right. But he STOPS! Now he's turning his back on Cartier. Calder is skating off the ice! I can't believe it! NEAL CALDER IS SKAT- ING OFF THE ICE!

When Neal got to the bench, he started to sit down. But Grady Hall's look stopped him. The coach's eyes burned deep into Neal's face. "Go to the locker room, Calder," Coach Hall said. "You're through."

Table Talk **10**

Neal Calder finished the season and the first play-off round sitting on the bench. Coach Hall wasn't about to play anyone who ran from fights. But even without Neal's help, Oakland got by Portland four games to two. And Los Angeles beat Seattle in four of five games. Finally, the Lions came to Oakland to play the Traders for the Gilbert Cup. The first team to win four games would take the Gilbert Cup home.

The night before the opening game, the Blairs and the Calders had dinner together. As always, hockey took over the table talk. But this time, the four friends had a lot of catching up to do.

"We've been following your career in the *Oakland Tribune*," Amy told Eddie. "You're doing well. Are you happy there?"

Eddie put down his fork and smiled. "It's not the Traders. But it's OK." Then he looked at Amy and Neal. "Never mind me," he said. "How are things going with you two?"

Amy didn't answer. Neal had to be the one to talk about his problems. So he did.

"Things aren't going too well for me, Eddie," he said. "You probably know that Coach Hall's got me riding the bench now. I'm thinking pretty hard about getting out of hockey."

Eddie stopped smiling. "Don't do anything silly," he said. "Is that Moyer fight still giving you a hard time?"

Neal nodded. "I don't think I'll ever be able to beat it. In fact, it's getting worse. At first, I thought I was only afraid of hurting someone else," he went on. "But now I'm beginning to wonder if it isn't more than that. I think I'm afraid that next time the guy on the bottom will be *me*. And the fear—no matter what it's about—is making me sick."

"You're too good a hockey player to be talking like that," Eddie said. He looked hard at

Neal. "You can make it all the way to the NHL and you know it. But not with those thoughts on your mind."

"I can't help what I think," Neal said.

"Don't tell me that," Eddie answered. "And don't think you're the only one who gets scared. I'm afraid each time I go out on the ice. The fear I feel wants to eat me up. But I won't let it! I won't let it keep me from playing the game I love. You don't have to let it stop you either."

"Maybe you're right," Neal said.

"No maybe about it," Eddie returned. "Show people you can handle yourself. And pretty soon no one will want to fight you." Eddie stopped for a minute. Then he said, "Why not start tomorrow?"

"I'll give it a try," Neal said. "But first I've got to handle one more problem."

Eddie asked, "What's that?"

"I've got to find a way to get off the bench," Neal answered.

The next day, the coliseum arena was jammed with people. Three of them—Carol Blair, Maria Blair, and Amy Hansen-Calder—sat together in front-row seats. Just before the face-off, Carol took Amy's hand. She said, "Eddie asked me to tell you something. He said to tell you that no matter what happens out there today, Neal is his best friend."

Amy looked surprised. "I already know that," she said. "And Eddie is Neal's best friend. I'm sure you both know that too."

"Let's be sure we remember it," Carol said. "No matter what."

Amy started to ask Carol a question. But just then the horn sounded. Then "The Star-Spangled Banner" rang out. After that the referee dropped the puck. And the fight for the Gilbert Cup began.

From the first moment play began, there was only one player on the Lions' team to watch. It was Eddie Blair. He was all over the ice, checking hard and keeping the Traders well away from the Lions' net. His skates flashed while his stick beat open a road for the puck. Eddie Blair put into play some of the best moves of his career. But Neal watched Eddie's fine work from the bench for the whole first period.

Early in the second period, Eddie nailed an Oakland defenseman with a clean, hard check. The Trader dropped in his tracks and had to be carried off the ice. Neal Calder took his place. And it was like training camp all over again.

From the very second that Neal touched a skate to the ice, Eddie Blair dogged him. He checked him, pushed him, and banged him with his stick. Eddie went everywhere Neal moved. And he did everything he could to get Neal burning mad at him.

It worked. Just as it had worked during training. Finally Neal blew up. And forgot about everything. He forgot about hurting or getting hurt. He forgot about Bad Boy Moyer. All he knew was the need to fight back. He swung at Eddie Blair from somewhere on the other side of fear.

Up in the press box, Manuel Lazar shouted above the noise:

Calder nails Blair with two quick rights. Blair comes right back with a smashing left. Another left. Calder now with a left. And a right again. These two players are really after each other.

The linesmen finally pulled Neal and Eddie away from each other when the two players fell to the ice, both still swinging. As Eddie stood up, he smiled at Neal through a fat lip. "There, now," he said. "That wasn't so hard, was it?"

Neal looked hard into Eddie's eyes. Then he broke out laughing.

With the fight behind him, Neal Calder played hockey like no one ever played it before. Each time he came off the bench, he brought trouble to the Lions. Every game he showed them something different. A quick move. Then an easy goal from in close. Then a screaming goal shot from center ice. And on and on.

Neal made hard, smashing body checks on every play. And when fights came his way, his quick hands ended them fast. For the first time since his fight with Bad Boy Moyer, he was in control again. With Neal showing the way, the Oakland Traders won the Gilbert Cup in only four games.

Hockey Is a Tough Game! 12

The day after the Traders had won the Gilbert Cup, Neal got a phone call. It came from Boston. The voice on the other end of the line was music to Neal's ears:

"Neal this is Harvey Warner of the Boston Bruins. I'd like to talk with you about a contract. Are you interested?"

"You *know* I am," Neal said.

"Good," Warner returned. "I'll be coming out your way next week. I'll call you when I get there."

"Great," Neal said. When he put down the phone, he let out a shout. Just then Amy walked in the door. She looked at Neal. "What's the matter?"

"I'm going to be a Boston Bruin," Neal said with a big smile. Amy let out a shout of her own. Then she and Neal danced around the living room. When they fell into chairs, they decided to call the Blairs and tell them the good news.

"That's great," Carol and Eddie both said. Then Eddie went on. "I've got a little good news of my own. Right after we lost the Gilbert Cup last night, the L.A. Lions decided that they needed a new coach. Guess who it's going to be?"

"Coach Eddie Blair!" Amy and Neal spoke together. Then Amy said, "Let's have a party!"

"Good idea," Eddie said. "But first, how would you and Neal like to go to one more hockey game? Maria is in a game at Iceland over on Milvia Street at four o'clock."

Amy answered for both of them. "Can't think of anything we would rather do. We'll meet you at the rink."

A little after four o'clock, the Blairs and the Calders were watching junior hockey at its best. Girls and boys raced over the ice, trying to put their own team in the lead. Maria Blair made a break for the other team's goal. It looked like she might score. But as she neared the net, a boy from the other team skated into her. Both kids fell down. Then they grabbed each other and rolled over and over on the ice. Trying to hold back a smile, the referee shouted, "Two minutes each for fighting!"

In the stands, the Blairs and the Calders laughed. Some things never change. Eddie reached out and tapped Neal on the arm.

"Do you remember what I told you?" he asked.

Neal smiled and nodded. Then, together, they said, *"Hockey is a tough game."*

In the penalty box, Maria Blair waited to get back on the ice.